TRUMP THE GREAT!
GOD'S END-TIME VESSEL

TRUMP THE GREAT!

--THE--
45TH & 47TH
PRESIDENT OF THE UNITED STATES.
GOD'S END-TIME VESSEL

PASTOR CLIFF MCANTHONY

TRUMP THE GREAT!

--THE--
45TH & 47TH
PRESIDENT OF UNITED STATES
GOD'S END-TIME VESSEL

BY PASTOR CLIFF MCANTHONY

For distribution of this book, contact the author:

Telephone/WhatsApp: +17819132528

Email: pclpressus@gmail.com

Follow Author on:

YouTube: Cliff McAnthony

Facebook: Cliff McAnthony

Table of Contents

Chapter 9

Chapter 10

Introduction

I have often received revelations from God through dreams about future events in my life, that of others, and of nations. This book is about God's revelations to me about President Donald J. Trump, the 45th and 47th president of the United States. I have written this book because of what God said to me in November 2016 that keeps reechoing in my ears. On Thursday morning November 3, 2016, the week before the presidential election between Donald Trump and Hillary Clinton, God said to me; "Cliff, I showed you such a great revelation about America and you did nothing about it? What else will I show you, for you to know that Trump is the president of the United States?" Well, the rest is history, Trump was elected the 45th president of the United States of America in 2016.

Just like God asked me in 2016, what else will I show you for you to know that Trump is the president of the United States of America? He really did show me something else and I know for certain that President Trump is the 47th president of the United States come November 2024. God's question to me in 2016, "Cliff, I showed you such a great revelation about America and you did nothing about it?" keeps reechoing in my ears. I do not know with certainty what God wants me to do about these revelations. However, I could at least write a book about them; most importantly before it comes to pass so that people would know that God truly rules in the affairs of men and gives the kingdoms to whoever He chooses.

1

Daniel 4:17

This matter is by the decree of the watchers, and the demand by the word of the holy ones: to the intent that the living may know that the most High ruleth in the kingdom of men, and giveth it to whomsoever he will, and setteth up over the basest of men.

This book also sheds light on God's purpose for choosing President Donald Trump at this time. We are in the end time and God has started His last work of revival and preparation for His imminent return to rescue His children. Revivals of this magnitude and epoch-changing events never take place without the involvement of a powerful government authority. Bible history attests to this: for God to rescue the children of Israel from Egypt through epoch-changing events that marked the end of Egypt's reign as a superpower, He raised up Pharaoh who had a hardened heart suitable to achieve His purpose. God also raised up the likes of King Josiah in Israel to propagate His desired revivals as seen throughout the Scripture.

1 Kings 13:1-2

And, behold, there came a man of God out of Judah by the word of the Lord unto Bethel: and Jeroboam stood by the altar to burn incense. And he cried against the altar in the word of the Lord, and said, O altar, altar, thus saith the Lord; Behold, a child shall be born unto the house of David, Josiah by name; and upon thee shall he offer the priests of the high places that burn incense upon thee, and men's bones shall be burnt upon thee.

This book focuses on the most significant and parallel reflection of God's purpose for choosing President Trump. Before Jesus Christ came in the flesh, God raised up a world leader, King

Cyrus, to rebuild Jerusalem. This was done because according to God's words Jesus the Messiah will be born in Israel. To prepare for His first coming God raised up King Cyrus who rebuilt Jerusalem. We are at the end time and Jesus' second coming is imminent. According to God's words, Jesus must return physically to Jerusalem and God raised up another world leader like that in Isaiah 45; the 45th president of the United States of America, who once again restored Jerusalem in readiness for Jesus' second coming.

Chapter 1
The Dream of About 10/11

God has often given me revelations through dreams about future events in my life, that of others and of nations. Before I proceed with all that God showed me about President Trump and the 2016, 2020, and 2024 elections. I would like to share just one revelation that God gave me through a dream about a future event in my life in 2005.

In the year 2004, I was going through financial hardship in Nigeria. Prior to that period, I was an international businessman with multiple store locations. To cut a long story short, I lost everything. At the time, two of my brothers, Gabe, and Benny, lived with me in a rented three-bedroom apartment in Lagos. I could no longer pay my rent and my landlord was closing in on me through the court, and eviction got closer with each passing day. My brothers had to move in with friends. I remained in the sinking ship (my apartment) not having where to go and no one to call on for financial assistance.

One evening in my bedroom, the whole weight of my hopeless situation dawned on me, and fear gripped me. I was about to be homeless! I realized that the only one who could help me out of my mess was God. Being honest with myself, I knew that I had no right or justification whatsoever to call on God for help. Before that moment on that fateful evening, I do not remember ever going to church once on my own as an adult, not even once a year on crossover nights as most sinners do. I lived a sinful life and all I did was driven by self-will, I never considered God. Despite my godless lifestyle, God showed me great signs and even spoke to me audibly at one point to draw my attention to Him. Things which I will not go into in this book. However, I never heeded His call but continued with my worldly lifestyle and worldly pursuits.

Proverbs 15:8-9

The sacrifice of the wicked is an abomination to the LORD: but the prayer of the upright is his delight. The way of the wicked is an abomination unto the LORD: but he loveth him that followeth after righteousness.

Proverbs 28:9

He that turneth away his ear from hearing the law, even his prayer shall be abomination.

Knowing that I had no right to call on God for help, knowing that He would not hear me, and realizing that I had done God great evil by continually rejecting Him despite His goodness and manifestations to me, the full weight of my guilt became much heavier than that of my hopeless situation and fears. It overwhelmed me, and I burst into tears. I wept uncontrollably, repenting, and apologizing to God for my wickedness against Him. I wept and prayed prayers of repentance from that evening into the night, I cried a bucket of tears. I cannot tell how long this lasted, but it was until I could almost literally, if not literally, feel the hand of Jesus tapping me gently at my back, saying, My son, it is enough, I have forgiven you. Afterwards, I destroyed my pornographic, worldly movies, and rap music VCDs & CDs, and I trashed my marijuana and alcohol that was in the house. The next day I looked for a Bible-believing church and joined them, and that was the start of my true Christian journey!

The Lord showed me great mercy afterwards and rescued me from my hopeless situation and fears just at the nick of time. While in this dire circumstance, a Pastor friend, whom I had not seen or spoken with in a long time, called me to ask if I knew anyone who was looking for accommodation. He said that he and his wife were about to travel abroad and wanted someone in need of accommodation to look after their property while they were gone. I told them that I knew someone and would bring him the next day. When I got there the next day, he was surprised that I came alone and to learn that I was the one in need of accommodation. They were pleased to hand over to me the fully furnished home. I was still in the process of moving my things when my landlord got the eviction order and seized the apartment with some of my belongings in it. Glory to God Almighty for His mercies!

At the new place I had no job or business and was sustained miraculously by God, details of which I will not go into in this book. I learned to trust God for everything and to allow His will to preside over mine since the day I repented and became born again.

John 3:1-7

There was a man of the Pharisees, named Nicodemus, a ruler of the Jews: The same came to Jesus by night, and said unto him, Rabbi, we know that thou art a teacher come from God: for no man can do these miracles that thou doest, except God be with him. Jesus answered and said unto him, Verily, verily, I say unto thee, Except a man be born again, he cannot see the kingdom of God. Nicodemus saith unto him, How can a man be born when he is old? can he enter the second time into his mother's womb, and be born? Jesus answered, Verily, verily, I say unto thee, Except a man be born of water and of the Spirit, he cannot enter into the kingdom of God. That which is born of the flesh is flesh; and that which is born of the Spirit is spirit. Marvel not that I said unto thee, Ye must be born again.

When my father's friend and brother in Christ, Mr. Eleazer Unamba, heard of my financial condition, he sent for me to know what it would cost for me to revive my business to help. I took Mr. Eleazer's offer of help to God in prayers. God told me not to accept the offer because He was doing a new thing in my life, and I will see it.

Isaiah 43:18-19

Remember ye not the former things, neither consider the things of old. Behold, I will do a new thing; now it shall spring forth; shall ye not know it? I will even make a way in the wilderness, and rivers in the desert.

Then the next year, 2005, I felt that the best thing for me was to travel out of the country because starting life in Nigeria from scratch was a very difficult endeavor. I prayed to God and in a dream, He gave me five countries - the US, UK, Canada, France, and the Bahamas, and asked me to choose one, promising that He would grant me the visa.

I called my mother who lived in a different State, knowing that she has the grace to hear from God expressly. I told her of

8

my desire to travel out of Nigeria and asked her to pray and ask God for His will concerning it. I did not tell her my dream. When she got back to me, she said that God told her to ask me to choose one and He will grant me the visa. This confirmed what God said to me and I set off to seek to travel out of the country.

Around April or May 2005, God spoke to me in a dream. He said that I should not worry, that my travel would be on 10/11. In Nigeria, the day is written before the month, and since the year was not given, I assumed it to be the same year. I was very hopeful that God would do something about my travel on the 10th of November 2005. When this date came and passed without anything happening, I reasoned that I probably did not understand what the dream meant and discarded the dream.

The next year 2006, I went to a stock brokerage firm where I used to invest when I was in business, to invest for a neighbor friend of mine, Mr. Oguguo. The manager, who made the investments for me, knowing my financial situation, offered me a job in the company. I turned his offer down, despite my financial distress; because God asked me to forget former things because He was doing a new thing. I asked him to employ my younger brother Gabe, who had worked with me in business before it collapsed. I assured him that Gabe would be of more value to him than I would, but he refused and said that it was me he wanted. I told him that he could not have me and left. I left his office and got on a bus, heading to my next destination. As I was getting down from the bus, God spoke to me and asked me to go back and take the job because it was for me, and for a purpose. I turned back and when I got there, I told him what God said to me. He said that he would not be surprised if God said so, because something told him in his spirit that I belonged in the company. He asked me to bring my resume the next Monday for employment, to which I asked, "what of my brother"? He said, "bring him along". We both got hired the same day.

Later, in that same year, I got a letter from the American Embassy regarding an immigrant visa application I had made. I continued to correspond with the Embassy while working for the brokerage company. God granted me speedy promotion in the job, and I became a manager in April of 2007. On May 29th, the same year I got my visa to America. I concluded that God used the job to sustain me until my visa was granted.

I planned to resign from my job to immigrate to the US on June 30th, 2007. When I informed the CEO of the company of my intentions to resign, to relocate to the US, he said; "Don't resign, we will keep you and you will work for us from there". Because I just became a manager a couple of months prior, I had to postpone my traveling indefinitely until I was able to organize my team so that I could manage them from the US. After organizing my team, I confirmed my ticket to travel to the US in October of 2007.

There was a vigil service in our church the Friday before the week of my travel and as I was walking to church for the vigil service that night, I heard God call out to me, asking; "Do you remember 10/11?" I was almost in a frozen state. I never told anyone about the dream about 10/11 and I had totally disregarded and forgotten the dream since the 10th of November 2005. Without considering or remember it, I had confirmed my flight ticket to leave Nigeria the coming week Wednesday, October 10th, to arrive in the US on Thursday the 11th. When I arrived in the US the date was 10/11/2007 because in America the month is written before the day. In Nigeria 10/11 made sense and in America, it made perfect sense too! The arrival date stamped on my passport and my green card is 10/11/2007 just as God told me in a dream in 2005. God worked it out, using the job He asked me to take and without my consciousness of the dream, it came to pass exactly as God said to me in the dream I had in 2005.

Chapter 2
Revelation Of A Future Nigerian President

I do not know the full reasons why God chose to show me things about the governments of nations. Nonetheless, I know that it is far beyond political reasons. I know it is beyond politics because I am apolitical in nature. Therefore, the full reasons must be beyond politics. God has shown me things about the nations; Nigeria, the United States, and Russia.

In 2014 God showed me a dream, and in this dream, I was told that my brother won the presidency of Nigeria. I was taken to the place where the newly elected Nigerian president was giving a press conference. When I got there, there was a huge crowd and I could not see my brother, the newly elected president. The crowd did not allow me to get close but when I told them that the president was my brother everyone quickly gave way to me. When I got to the front, there were metal barricades restricting the press from coming close. I could now see the newly elected president as he gave his speech with so many press mics on the podium. I stood there confused, as I held the barricade because I could not recognize the man who won the election, and who was supposed to be my brother.

While still wondering, he spotted me. As soon as he saw me, he stopped his speech. He ran quickly towards me saying; "My brother, my brother" as onlookers wondered what was going on.

He got to where I was, removed the barricade, and hugged me as he continued to call me his brother. I was surprised that he knew me very well as his brother even though I did not know him. I kept on wondering as we hugged each other, and then I woke up.

Fast forward to 2021, seven years later, I traveled to Nigeria for a Christian conference. At that conference, I met and recognized this man I saw in my dream who won the Nigerian presidential election. He is currently a Senator in Nigeria, and guess what, he is my brother indeed! He is a true Christian and my brother in Christ. Just like I was told in the dream that my brother won the presidential election. If he were to win the presidential election today, it would be rightfully said that my brother won the election.

This dream came to me about a couple of weeks after Narendra Modi won the election in India to become the Prime Minister. When I heard of Modi's victory and political carrier on BBC, I was perplexed by his political achievement. I pondered on how he was able to climb from the bottom to achieve this political landmark victory of defeating the Gandi family in India. Then I concluded that it could only be God, and that it was for a purpose. A few weeks later I had the dream about the Nigerian president. I also found out that this upcoming Nigerian president's political career is like that of Narendra Modi, the Prime Minister of India. The difference is that he has not yet attained the highest office in the land. I believe that when he becomes the president of Nigeria, he will also transform Nigeria and set it on the world stage like Narendra Modi is doing with India.

God reveals both present and future events to people of His

choice. It has always been the nature and pleasure of God to reveal His will and plans to human vessels of His choice.

Numbers 12:6

And he said, Hear now my words: If there be a prophet among you, I the LORD will make myself known unto him in a vision, and will speak unto him in a dream.

Amos 3:7

Surely the Lord GOD will do nothing, but he revealeth his secret unto his servants the prophets.

Chapter 3
Revelation About The 2016 US Presidential Election

I had a dream in 2016 about the US presidential elections when there were still about 11 candidates competing for the Republican nomination. In this dream, I understood that Donald Trump would be the Republican nominee and that the presidential election would be decided by the sitting Americans during elections. That is, those that do not usually participate in elections. Prior to this dream, I disliked Trump so much so that it bordered on hatred. I was confused about why God would choose a man like Trump to be the president of the United States. I also thought that it could have been Satan that showed me the dream. After sharing the dream with my family and a few others, I concluded that Trump had some kind of supernatural power backing him up. I also reasoned that if Trump lost the election, it would prove that Satan was the power behind him, and if he won, then, it must have been God.

Romans 13:1

Let every soul be subject unto the higher powers. For there is no power but of God: the powers that be are ordained of God.

1Kings 19:15-16

And the LORD said unto him, Go, return on thy way to the wilderness of Damascus: and when thou comest, anoint Hazael to be king over Syria: And Jehu the son of Nimshi shalt thou anoint to be king over Israel: and Elisha the son of Shaphat of Abelmeholah shalt thou anoint to be prophet in thy room.

Psalm 75:6-7

For promotion cometh neither from the east, nor from the west, nor from the south. But God is the judge: he putteth down one, and setteth up another.

Daniel 4:17

This matter is by the decree of the watchers, and the demand by the word of the holy ones: to the intent that the living may know that the most High ruleth in the kingdom of men, and giveth it to whomsoever he will, and setteth up over it the basest of men.

My Knowledge of Donald Trump:

Before I had this dream, I knew very little about Donald Trump. My knowledge of him was from his TV show, "The Apprentice". I hardly watched the show, though my coworkers at the time usually put it on at work. I neither liked him nor the show. I found him arrogant with his "You are fired!" attitude.

When he later declared his presidential candidacy, I thought he was just clowning around. I never took him seriously and was offended by the way he spoke. My preconception of him as arrogant added to my borderline hatred for him. It was grave enough to cause me to sin against God. I would call him a fool and then start to repent, asking God for forgiveness. I knew better not to call him or anyone a fool in that manner, but I could not help myself because of the disdain I had for him.

Matthew 5:22

"But I say unto you, That whosoever is angry with his brother without a cause shall be in danger of the judgment: and whosoever shall say to his brother, Raca, shall be in danger of the council: but whosoever shall say, Thou fool, shall be in danger of hell fire."

I used to say that other presidential candidates should not give the fool (Trump) attention, that he would eliminate himself with his own mouth. I continued to struggle with this name calling and as often as I fell, I repented. After much struggle I decided that the best thing to do was to distance myself from listening to Trump, to avoid sinning against God; to avoid His judgement. I avoided listening to him as much as I could and distanced myself from the 2016 politics to the best of my ability. I had never been interested in politics prior to the 2016 presidential race. I am apolitical in nature; it was Trump that drew my attention to politics. Even during the time of Obama's presidential race as the first potential black president, I gave little attention to politics. I have never participated in elections in America.

Despite the revelations God had given me about Trump and the 2016 presidential elections, I did not vote at all. Hate Trump or love him, he was the person that drew the attention of many Americans to politics. He became the face of politics in America till this day, since June 16, 2015, when he formally announced his candidacy.

My 2016 Dream About Trump and The Elections

In 2016 I had this dream about Trump when there were still 11 candidates running for the Republican presidential ticket, including Trump. In this dream, I was told that Trump wanted to see me. I wondered why Trump would want to see me and what business I could possibly have with him! Nonetheless, I went to see him.

When I got there, he was seated, with men dressed in black suits around him who must have been his bodyguards and his campaign crew. He offered me a seat beside him and said, "Cliff, I want you to campaign for me." I said "no, I cannot campaign for you". He then put his hand in his breast pocket and offered me a toothpick-like stick (I perceived in the dream that the toothpick signified a million dollars). I declined, saying "no, I cannot campaign for you, and moreover, I am apolitical in nature". He replied, "Cliff I am rewarding you handsomely and you won't campaign for me?". I responded, "how do I know you are rewarding me handsomely when I don't know what other candidates have to offer for the same position?" He pressed on saying, "okay" as he brought out another stick making it two. I insisted, "I cannot campaign for you even if you offered me your whole estate." After a second thought I said to him, "Let me go and pray about it and know what God has to say about it." He was very surprised that I would turn down such an offer to say I wanted to know what God had to say.

Then suddenly, still in the dream, I saw myself on a train going back home. I was standing by the train's door, reflecting on my conversation with Trump when I noticed two black men standing in my front. Instinctively, I thought to myself to ask the men what they thought about Trump, to know if I was the only person who thought he was unfit to be the president of the United States. When I asked the one to my left, he went on ranting against Trump just like me, categorically saying that he was not fit to be the president. Next, I asked the one on my right and to my surprise, he spoke pleasantly about Trump. He said, "America will later say that Trump is one of the best presidents, or is the best president that America ever had." I was astonished at his statement and wondered how anyone could say something good about Trump and go further to think that he would be the best president ever. To break the opinion deadlock, I turned to ask the woman sitting further on my right side by the entry door. Unfortunately, I woke up without asking her.

My Interpretation of The Dream

Through this dream, I clearly understood that Trump would become the Republican nominee. In the dream, the two black men standing by me in the train represented what was ahead– the 2016 election. There were two parties voting: those against Trump, and those for Trump. By this, I knew that Trump would triumph over the other ten candidates running for the Republican presidential ticket and that the presidential election would be between Hilary Clinton and Donald Trump.

The dream also revealed that the presidential election would be a stalemate and would be decided by the sitting Americans (i.e., those who do not usually participate in elections). The two black men represented the usual voting population; half was against Trump and half was for Trump. The woman sitting on my right by the entry door of the train, whom I turned to, to break the deadlock between the two men before I woke up from the dream represented those who do not usually participate in elections.

Having this understanding of the dream, I knew that the election could go either way depending on who the sitting population stood up to support. However, I could not understand why God would choose a man like Trump to be the president of the United States. I also thought Satan could have showed me the dream. I shared the dream with my family, co-workers, and a few others, concluding that Trump had some kind of supernatural power backing him up. I settled on the argument that if Trump lost the election, then Satan was responsible for the dream, and if he won, it was from God and God's power was backing him up.

Romans 13:1

Let every soul be subject unto the higher powers. For there is no power but of God: the powers that be are ordained of God.

1Kings 19:15-16

And the LORD said unto him, Go, return on thy way to the wilderness of Damascus: and when thou comest, anoint Hazael to be king over Syria: And Jehu the son of Nimshi shalt thou anoint to be king over Israel: and Elisha the son of Shaphat of Abelmeholah shalt thou anoint to be prophet in thy room.

Psalm 75:6-7

For promotion cometh neither from the east, nor from the west, nor from the south. But God is the judge: he putteth down one, and setteth up another.

Daniel 4:17

This matter is by the decree of the watchers, and the demand by the word of the holy ones: to the intent that the living may know that the most High ruleth in the kingdom of men, and giveth it to whomsoever he will, and setteth up over it the basest of men.

Chapter 4

The Second Visitation From God On The 2016 US Presidential Election

By the time I had the second visitation of God about the 2016 US presidential elections, Donald Trump had emerged as the Republican nominee contesting against Hilary Clinton, just as I expected, following the dream I had about the election. Nonetheless, I had remained skeptical about God's support for Trump, unable to understand why God would support a man like him. Going by my dream, I was convinced that there was a supernatural power behind Trump. Which power that was, whether God or Satan was my confusion. At this time, I waited anxiously for the election to be over in order to conclude on the power behind Trump.

Then on Thursday, November 3rd, 2016, the week before the presidential election, following overnight work duty, I was headed to drop my clients off at their day program with a coworker. While at the stop light, between Andover and Lawrence in Massachusetts, I heard a distinct voice speaking to me in my heart, saying; "Cliff, I showed you a great revelation about this nation and you did nothing about it. What else will I show you for you to know that Trump is the president of the United States?" In response, I said, "Probably, if you show me a dream with Trump holding the flag of the United States with 45 written on it, then I will know that he is the 45th president of the United States." Even at that I would just tell people my dream and leave them to come up with their own interpretation. As soon as I finished responding, I was in awe as I could feel the voice leaving. Immediately, I realized that I was not communicating with my own mind as I could feel a presence leaving me. As I was in awe, immediately without any gap in communication my client sitting at the back of the van asked me; "Cliff who won the election last night?" I was shocked! He could have asked the staff sitting beside him, but he did not. Why me, who was driving? Right then, I knew that it was God who just spoke to me because in the mouth of two or three witnesses shall every word be established.

2Corinthian 13:1

This is the third time I am coming to you. In the mouth of two or three witnesses shall every word be established.

To be sure of the election he was referring to since I was not really into politics and thought that there could have been a senate race the night before, I asked; "Which election?" He said, Hilary and Trump. This conversation happened on Thursday morning, five days before the presidential election! I told him that Trump won the elections. He said, "NO! Trump cannot win!" I told him that I had received the information on the election just before he asked. My other coworker Jacob exclaimed that Trump could never win the election. He also said that if Trump won, he would move to Canada. I told him to pack his things once he got home, move to Canada, and not wait till Tuesday the following week, the day of the elections. The rest is history!

My Prayers for God's People

God's visitation to me that Thursday morning cleared all doubts in me, totally changed my position, and sealed my conviction about Trump. That same day, I texted a church member who is an ardent Democrat, informing him that Trump has won the election. He texted back, "hahaha!". I responded, "I hope still laugh on Tuesday." I did not tell him that Trump was going to win the election, but that Trump had already won. That was how sure and confident I was about the outcome of the election. Then on Saturday before Tuesday's presidential election, while at work, I saw the election polls on CNN go down even more against Trump. It was so dire that all that was left to do was to make Hilary Clinton the president of the United States without an election. When I got home that day, I went to God in prayers, with a broken heart and prayed earnestly. I was not praying because I had doubt, but because I could see the depth of the hopeless situation that Trump was in, which God wanted to turn around. I could clearly see the magnitude of what God was about to do. That day, I prayed as I had never prayed before, and my prayer was, "God, if You make this happen in America, I will go to any length to open the eyes of your people, for your people are blind." Well, the rest is history!

2Chronicles 7:14

If my people, which are called by my name, shall humble themselves, and pray, and seek my face, and turn from their wicked ways; then will I hear from heaven, and will forgive their sin, and will heal their land.

The 2016 presidential election between Hillary Clinton and Donald Trump was decided exactly as God revealed it to me. The

Almighty God was able to use Trump to rally the discouraged voter base to rise and vote him into office.

Psalm 110:3

Thy people shall be willing in the day of thy power,...

Donald Trump was the person who drew the attention of many Americans to politics and gave courage to the discouraged voter base. He was able to pull this off because God was on his side and by His power made the people willing. Since June 16th, 2016, the day he announced his candidacy, he became the face of politics in America.

Chapter 5
Dream About 2020 and 2024 US Presidential Election

On Thursday, November 3rd, 2016, five days before the presidential election, God asked me; "What else will I show you for you to know that Trump is the president of the United States?" God further revealed more on August 15th, 2020, about the 2020 and 2024 presidential elections.

In this dream I was in a living room, watching the 2020 presidential debate between President Trump and Joe Biden. The debate did not go well for Trump, Biden won in all subject matters and the whole crowd was applauding him as if no one there was in support of President Trump. Suddenly, President Trump came in and kind of slumped on the couch opposite where I was seated, feeling demoralized. I went up to him to encourage him and said he should remember the 2016 election between him and Hillary. No one gave him a chance, the polls were terrible, and the only thing left to do was to declare Hilary Clinton the president of the United States without an election. Notwithstanding, God's word prevailed. I told him not to worry about all that had happened, that the election would decide; all that matters is what God says. As I was encouraging him, he said to me "No, no, no, no, Hilary Clinton's own was different, forget it. I know I've lost the election." I told him to trust God, that it is what God says that really matters." However, Trump did not take my comfort and encouragement.

Fast-forward and suddenly, it was election time, as if the scene was removed and a new scene had come, like in a movie. The new scene was in Massachusetts. We could see on TV, people trooping out in thousands, voting for President Trump to the point that the ballot box got filled and they said, bring another. Trump was astonished, became lively again and exclaimed; "If it is like this in Massachusetts, what is it like then in the red States?" He then stood up and was like a giant. He grabbed my hand and said, "Let's go!". As we came out of the house, we saw a long line of black voters queued up to vote against Trump. He said to me, "Cliff, what have I done wrong to your people despite all my care and efforts to help them?". I asked him not to worry about them because they lacked understanding.

We continued walking to where his car was parked. It was a beautiful sports car. When we got to the car, he opened the hood, put back one of the battery head terminals, and hit it with something to tighten it, as we were about to enter the car. Suddenly, a black guy in dirty greasy mechanic clothing called out to Trump to give him a ride because he could not get transport back home since he closed work. As I was wondering in my heart what Trump would do, without any hesitation, he said, "Come on in." I was shocked that he would agree to give the black guy in greasy dirty mechanic clothes, a ride in his spotlessly beautiful clean sports car. Then in my heart, I said, "Trump is really humble, contrary to my previous thought that he is arrogant." Then, Trump directed him to go to the back seat as I sat in the front seat. Then Trump brought out a toothpick-like stick from his breast pocket, identical to the ones he offered me in 2016. With a smile, he gave it to me saying, "Cliff, this is for your amusement." As we were about to drive off, I woke up.

I was thrilled about this dream as I could see that God was with President Trump for a second term. More so, for the fact that I already knew that Trump has a second term since 2016. I interpreted the dream to mean that President Trump was going to win the 2020 presidential election against Biden. I spoke with all assurance that President Trump was going to win the election. For the first time, I participated in the US election and voted for President Trump. I was shocked when President Trump lost the election.

The dream was clear and God's revelations to me through dreams usually come to pass. I wondered what could have gone wrong. When I decided to carefully examine the dream again, I realized that my interpretation was wrong. I was quick to believe that the dream meant President Trump was going to win the 2020 presidential election without paying attention to the details. I was not mindful to interpret the dream accurately because of my prior knowledge of the reality of President Trump's second term. Here is an excerpt from my Facebook post in 2016, shortly after the election that proves my prior knowledge of the certainty of President Trump's second term in office.

Excerpt From My Facebook Post in 2016

Folks, it is unscriptural and theologically inaccurate to say that the president of any nation is not instituted by God. It is also a misinterpretation of the Scripture to say that King Saul was chosen by the people and not by God. The people of Israel rejected God, but God chose their king, read (1Samuel 9:15-17).

As Christians the Scripture is our ultimate source of authority and source of reference for truth irrespective of our personal opinions. The Bible made it very clear that "all authorities" are instituted by God (Romans 13:1-2). "All" includes President Donald J. Trump.

In the Scripture, God asked Isaiah to go and anoint Hazael as king over Syria (the enemies of Israel) and anoint Jehu as king over Israel, read (1Kings 19:15-16). God raised Pharaoh as king over Egypt (Romans 9:17). God instituted Nebuchadnezzar as king of Babylon – Iraq (Jeremiah 27:5-8).

King Cyrus and King Darius, the Persian Kings (Iran) were also instituted by God (2Chronicles 36:22-23, Ezra 1:1-2). God also used kind Cyrus and Darius to rebuild the Temple of God in Jerusalem (Ezra 4:3; 5:13; 6:12-14). This tells us that God can also use an ungodly king or president for the good of His people.

You really don't have to accept this statement that:

America will later say that Trump is one of the best presidents, if not the best president that America ever had, especially Christians. President J. Trump is sent by God for the good of America.

However, please note it down for the future. I did not vote in this election. My whole duty was to pray for the will of God to prevail, and that is all I did. I am apolitical in nature and not affiliated with any political party, so by default, I am called "Independent" but I am not from a political standpoint. I am a Christian and the Bible is my ultimate source of authority, and I only view things from God's perspective and speak on the authority of the Scripture.

Here Is Another Revelation:

President J. Trump's reign will be likened to those of King Cyrus and Darius. God will use him to rebuild His kingdom in America. Note – "Cyrus and Darius" if you have spiritual understanding, you will know what this means, otherwise, God willing, I will explain in the future. God bless you.

The Correct Interpretation Of The Dream on August 15, 2020

Fast-forward and suddenly, it was election time, as if the scene was removed and a new scene had come, like in a movie. The new scene was in Massachusetts. We could see on TV, people trooping out in thousands, voting for President Trump to the point that the ballot box got filled and they said, bring another. Trump was astonished, became lively again and exclaimed; "If it is like this in Massachusetts, what is it like then in the red States?"

1. The fast-forward scene change shows that the new winning scene where President Trump was doing well in Massachusetts and the ballot boxes were getting filled was not the 2020 election, but a future election. The 'loss' he was referring to in this dream was fulfilled in 2020, when President Trump lost the election to President Biden. The election to come, where the voter turnout was going in his favor is the 2024 presidential election.

2. Massachusetts shall be a sign that God is behind President Trump. He will do very well in Massachusetts in 2024, to the astonishment of many. He will record an outstanding performance in Massachusetts regardless of the outcome. However, from what I saw in the dream, President Trump will most likely carry the day in Massachusetts.

We continued walking to where his car was parked. It was a beautiful sports car. When we got to the car, he opened the hood, put back one of the battery head terminals, and hit it with something to tighten it, as we were about to enter the car. …. As we were about to drive off, I woke up.

1. The sports car represents President Trump's presidential office. The car being packed shows that his presidential office was packed (suspended) for a while (2021 to 2024)

2. The battery heads represent President Trump's two terms in office. One of the battery heads that was removed shows that his second term was intentionally suspended by God. This is true irrespective of the circumstances that led to it (whether it was through election fraud or a clean win) God's hand was in it because He has this whole thing planned out. All things work together for good.

Romans 8:28

And we know that all things work together for good to them that love God, to them who are the called according to his purpose.

3. "Put back one of the battery heads terminals, … and as we were about to drive off, I woke up." this means that God will put back President Trump's second term that He suspended, and kick start his presidential office come 2024. His 2024 presidential office will surely drive off!

This is the perfect interpretation of this dream I had on August 15, 2020, about the 2020 and 2024 presidential elections. Without a shadow of doubt President Trump will be elected back to office come November 2024. I said this to people in 2021 when I got the understanding and the right interpretation of the dream. I declared in 2021 that President Trump would run for a second term long before he announced his entrance into the 2024 presidential race on November 15, 2022. His entrance into the presidential race has come to pass, and so will his reelection into office come to pass. President Trump will surely be reelected into office come November 2024.

Chapter 6
Reason For The Great Battles Against President Trump

It is needless to start naming the political battles and witch-hunts that President Trump is up against. It is all over mainstream and social media. Most Americans and the world at large are aware of them. The causeless attacks and battles against President Trump are unprecedented. No one has ever seen such unjust malicious attacks, and blackmailing against anyone in the United States of America, not to talk of a sitting president nor an ex-president of the United States. President Trump faced these relentless, reckless, political, causeless attacks as a sitting president of the United States. And now much more as an ex-president and a presidential political opponent in the United States. No president in the history of America has come close to experiencing what he has suffered and is still suffering. The political persecution against him is unfathomable because it is a persecution from hell. It is not just political but most importantly spiritual.

The battle against President Trump is a battle between light and darkness. It is a battle between good and evil, it is a battle between God and Satan. The battle is not about President Trump, the battle is much larger than him. It is just as Trump said, "I am just standing in their way." The battle is truly between God and Satan, good and evil, light and darkness. President Trump just happened to be the man God found to stand in the gap.

Ezekiel 22:30

And I sought for a man among them, that should make up the hedge, and stand in the gap before Me for the land, that I should not destroy it: but I found none.

Fortunately, this time around the Lord found a man in the person of President Trump. That is why we are witnessing this massive scale of causeless, unjust, relentless, reckless, political attacks and humiliation against one man; he must be stopped at all costs! It is like, it is a matter of life and death; of course, it is a matter of life and death. However, only those who are spiritually minded and understand times and seasons can discern it. We are in the end time and President Trump is a vessel chosen by God as a battle axe in His hand to hew down and to reset the trajectory of the world towards One World Order in readiness for the Anti-Christ. God intends to use President Trump to set the stage for the end-time revival and Christ's imminent return to rescue His own.

Isaiah 45:1-4,13

Thus saith the LORD to his anointed, to Cyrus (Trump), whose right hand I have holden, to subdue nations before him; and I will loose the loins of kings, to open before him the two leaved gates; and the gates shall not be shut; I will go before thee, and make the crooked places straight: I will break in pieces the gates of brass, and cut in sunder the bars of iron: And I will give thee the treasures of darkness, and hidden riches of secret places, that thou mayest know that I, the LORD, which call thee by thy name, am the God of Israel. For Jacob my servant's sake, and Israel mine elect, I have even called thee by thy name: I have surnamed thee, though thou hast not known me. I have raised him up in righteousness, and I will direct all his ways: he shall build my city, and he shall let go my captives, not for price nor reward, saith the LORD of hosts.

Why did God Choose President Trump?

We are in the end time and God has started His last work of revival and preparation for His Imminent return to rescue His children. Revivals of this magnitude and epoch-changing events never take place without the involvement of a powerful government authority. Biblical history attests to this throughout the Scripture. God raised up the likes of King Josiah in Israel to carry out His desired revivals as seen in the Scripture.

1 Kings 13:1-2

And, behold, there came a man of God out of Judah by the word of the Lord unto Bethel: and Jeroboam stood by the altar to burn incense. And he cried against the altar in the word of the Lord, and said, O altar, altar, thus saith the Lord; Behold, a child shall be born unto the house of David, Josiah by name; and upon thee shall he offer the priests of the high places that burn incense upon thee, and men's bones shall be burnt upon thee.

For this book, I will focus on the ones that are of the most significance or that mirror God's purpose for choosing President Trump and President Biden.

Before Jesus Christ came in the flesh, God raised up King Cyrus to rebuild Jerusalem. This was done according to what was written in God's word, that Jesus the Messiah will be born in Israel. To prepare for His first coming, God raised up King Cyrus.

Isaiah 45:1-6,13

Thus saith the LORD to his anointed, to Cyrus, whose right hand I have holden, to subdue nations before him; and I will loose the loins of kings, to open before him the two leaved gates; and the gates shall not be shut; I will go before thee, and make the crooked places straight: I will break in pieces the gates of brass, and cut in sunder the bars of iron: And I will give thee the treasures of darkness, and hidden riches of secret places, that thou mayest know that I, the LORD, which call thee by thy name, am the God of Israel. For Jacob my servant's sake, and Israel mine elect, I have even called thee by thy name: I have surnamed thee, though thou hast not known me. I am the LORD, and there is none else, there is no God beside me: I girded thee, though thou hast not known me: That they may know from the rising of the sun, and from the west, that there is none beside me. I am the LORD, and there is none else. I have raised him up in righteousness, and I will direct all his ways: he shall build my city, and he shall let go my captives, not for price nor reward, saith the LORD of hosts.

When it comes to service, God uses anyone to achieve His purpose. King Cyrus was not a Jew and did not know God. Nonetheless, God chose him to rebuild Jerusalem in preparation for the first coming of Jesus Christ. God said He called him by name and was the One that gave him his surname though he did not know Him. God has also called President Trump by his name and chosen him as a vessel, even though he does not know God. God has prepared him for this time and season. God has raised him up because He wants to restore righteousness in America to facilitate the ongoing end-time revival. God has raised him to change the trajectory of the world towards the One-World Order in readiness to usher in the Anti-Christ. The Holy Spirit working and restraining the unveiling of the Anti-Christ so that he will be revealed in his time and not before his time.

2 Theselonians 2:6-8

And now ye know what withholdeth that he might be revealed in his time. For the mystery of iniquity doth already work: only he (Holy Spirit) who now letteth will let, until he be taken out of the way (at rapture). And then shall that Wicked be revealed, whom the Lord shall consume with the Spirit of his mouth, and shall destroy with the brightness of his coming: Even him, whose coming is after the working of Satan with all power and signs and lying wonders, And with all deceivableness of unrighteousness in them that perish; because they received not the love of the truth, that they might be saved.

Satan is laboring hard in the world through his agents to usher in the Anti-Christ before his time because he wants to abort the last days' revival so that multitudes of people would be damned eternally in hell. The Holy Spirit is also working hard through vessels chosen by God and through His power to destroy the works of Satan and restrain the Anti-Christ from being ushered in before his time. The Holy Spirit is doing this to ensure an effective end-time revival ensues. President Trump happens to be one of these vessels of God, charged with significant end-time tasks.

God used President Trump in his first term in office to restore Jerusalem back as the capital of Israel just as He used King Cyrus. This was done in readiness for the second coming of Jesus Christ after the rapture for His millennial reign. Jesus must return to Israel as it is written in God's word and Israel must be fully restored with Jerusalem as its capital. Jesus will rule from Jerusalem, the center of the world as the capital of Israel. Therefore, Jerusalem must be restored, and God did it through President Trump because we are at the end time.

Acts 1:10-11

And while they looked stedfastly toward heaven as he went up, behold, two men stood by them in white apparel; Which also said, Ye men of Galilee, why stand ye gazing up into heaven? this same Jesus, which is taken up from you into heaven, shall so come in like manner as ye have seen him go into heaven.

Isaiah 2:2-4

And it shall come to pass in the last days, that the mountain of the LORD'S house shall be established in the top of the mountains, and shall be exalted above the hills; and all nations shall flow unto it. And many people shall go and say, Come ye, and let us go up to the mountain of the LORD, to the house of the God of Jacob; and he will teach us of his ways, and we will walk in his paths: for out of Zion shall go forth the law, and the word of the LORD from Jerusalem. And he shall judge among the nations, and shall rebuke many people: and they shall beat their swords into plowshares, and their spears into pruninghooks: nation shall not lift up sword against nation, neither shall they learn war any more.

Jeremiah 3:17

At that time they shall call Jerusalem the throne of the LORD; and all the nations shall be gathered unto it, to the name of the LORD, to Jerusalem: neither shall they walk any more after the imagination of their evil heart.

God used President Trump in his first term as president to change the judicial landscape in America. Here is a clearer picture of what God achieved through President Trump in the judicial system in his first term: The nine Supreme Court Justices are lifetime appointees of the president. Their appointment is either till they die or till they retire. A president could be in office for two terms and not change even one. President Trump changed three in his one term in office. Because of this achievement, the infamous half-a-century-old Roe vs Wade federal abortion law was overturned in America. God also used President Trump to remove the 1954 Johnson Amendment law that prohibits pastors from endorsing or opposing political candidates because of 501C. This law literally shuts the mouths of pastors from speaking the truth in their hearts in support or opposition against any political candidate. Through President Trump God gave pastors a voice again in America to educate their congregation to vote in the best interest of the church. God achieved much through President Trump for the good of America and the world. This is just to highlight a few things of great spiritual significance, in connection with God's end-time plans.

Chapter 7

God's Purpose For Raising Joseph Biden As President Of America

The Bible is the word of God and remains the Ultimate Source of Authority (USA) for all, both Christians and non-Christians. The Word of God applies to all and affects all regardless of their acceptance or rejection of the Bible. The Word of God is very clear that all authorities are instituted by God, whether good or bad. This includes that of President Joe Biden.

Romans 13:1

Let every soul be subject unto the higher powers. For there is no power but of God: the powers that be are ordained of God.

1Kings 19:15-16

And the LORD said unto him, Go, return on thy way to the wilderness of Damascus: and when thou comest, anoint Hazael to be king over Syria: And Jehu the son of Nimshi shalt thou anoint to be king over Israel: and Elisha the son of Shaphat of Abelmeholah shalt thou anoint to be prophet in thy room.

Psalm 75:6-7

For promotion cometh neither from the east, nor from the west, nor from the south. But God is the judge: he putteth down one, and setteth up another.

Daniel 4:17

This matter is by the decree of the watchers, and the demand by the word of the holy ones: to the intent that the living may know that the most High ruleth in the kingdom of men, and giveth it to whomsoever he will, and setteth up over it the basest of men.

The question one may ask is, of what purpose is Joe Biden's presidency in God's end-time plans? A president so corrupt and obviously anti-God in his policies and actions. A bloodthirsty man so hard-hearted in doing evil against humanity and his political opponent. The man that has sent over four hundred and fifty thousand (450,000) Ukrainians to the meat-grinder called the Ukrainian war. Who also caused the death of thousands of Russian soldiers and still thirsty for more blood through a senseless war that should never have happened. The man who sent over 46 billion US taxpayer dollars to fund a senseless war in Ukraine while many Americans who paid taxes are homeless and hungry. The one who has created a devastating humanitarian crisis all over America with his senseless open border policy and wrecked the US economy.

President Joe Biden that signed into law the Gender Affirming Care Act, which indoctrinates and groom innocent children in schools to affirm them the opposite gender of their imagination or an imaginary gender from hell. Then he goes for the kill, by poisoning them with hormone blockers and chopping off their God-given sex organs at birth even without parental consent. What purpose in the world does a man like this serve in God's end-time plan?

Romans 8:28

And we know that all things work together for good to them that love God, to them who are the called according to his purpose.

When God wanted to rescue the children of Israel from Egypt through epoch-changing events that marked the end of Egypt's oppression against His people Israel, and their reign as a superpower, He raised up Pharaoh who had a hardened heart suitable to achieve His purpose.

Exodus 9:16-18

And in very deed for this cause have I raised thee up, for to shew in thee my power; and that my name may be declared throughout all the earth. As yet exaltest thou thyself against my people, that thou wilt not let them go? Behold, to morrow about this time I will cause it to rain a very grievous hail, such as hath not been in Egypt since the foundation thereof even until now.

Romans 9:17

For the scripture saith unto Pharaoh, Even for this same purpose have I raised thee up, that I might shew my power in thee, and that my name might be declared throughout all the earth.

God wants to bring an end to the systematic oppression against His people and His word in America. He wants to obliterate the Deep State occult that is destroying righteousness in America and the world. God does not only want to drain the swamp of all the reptilian monsters and the rhinos in it, but He also literally wants to dry up the swamp. Hence, God raised up another Pharaoh; corrupt President Biden whose heart is hardened to do evil. His wicked plan to destroy millions of innocent children for generations through his Gender Affirming Care Act only helped to reveal the evil in him and his evil extremist Deep State occult ring. His relentless efforts to get rid of his political opponent by any corrupt means necessary have only helped to expose how deeply broken and corrupt America's government is. His relentless pursuit to destroy President Trump, his leading political opponent, has only helped to uncover and expose all the reptilians and rhinos that were not easily visible in the swamp. His relentless, reckless persecution of President Trump has exposed and will continue to expose most of the Deep State occult men and women who want to destroy America and hand it over to the devil. Now the American people and President Trump can clearly see even the micro-monsters that are hidden in the swamp.

Like I said earlier, God has this whole thing planned out, the reason why He suspended President Trump's second term and raised President Biden to expose all the Deep State swamp creatures, for eradication. The political arena in America will never be the same again once Trump gets back into office in 2024. God will use him and the American people to drain and dry up the swamp. The swampy creatures know this and that is why they have all joined forces together to fight President Trump because, to them, it is a matter of an existential threat.

Without a shadow of a doubt, President Trump will be elected back to office come November 2024. I made this known to people in 2021 when I got the understanding and the right interpretation of my August 15, 2020, dream. I declared in 2021 that President Trump would run for a second term long before he announced his entrance into the 2024 presidential race on November 15, 2022. His entrance into the presidential race has come to pass. His reelection into office will also come to pass as the Lord has shown me. President Trump will surely be reelected into office come November 2024.

Because of the evils of President Biden, there will be a political shake-up around the world especially in the Western world. Then, like King Josiah, President Trump will begin to purge the American political system of the reptilian monsters and rhinos of the Deep State with the help of the American people. This political shake-up will usher in a new era of government that will promote righteousness and enhance the ongoing end-time revival.

2Kings 23:3-20

And the king stood by a pillar, and made a covenant before the LORD, to walk after the LORD, and to keep his commandments and his testimonies and his statutes with all their heart and all their soul, to perform the words of this covenant that were written in this book. And all the people stood to the covenant. And the king commanded Hilkiah the high priest, and the priests of the second order, and the keepers of the door, to bring forth out of the temple of the LORD all the vessels that were made for Baal, and for the grove, and for all the host of heaven: and he burned them without Jerusalem in the fields of Kidron, and carried the ashes of them unto Bethel. And he put down the idolatrous priests, whom the kings of Judah had ordained to burn incense in the high places in the cities of Judah, and in the places round about Jerusalem; them also that burned incense unto Baal, to the sun, and to the moon, and to the planets, and to all the host of heaven. And he brought out the grove from the house of the LORD, without Jerusalem, unto the brook

Kidron, and burned it at the brook Kidron, and stamped it small to powder, and cast the powder thereof upon the graves of the children of the people. And he brake down the houses of the sodomites, that were by the house of the LORD, where the women wove hangings for the grove. And he brought all the priests out of the cities of Judah, and defiled the high places where the priests had burned incense, from Geba to Beersheba, and brake down the high places of the gates that were in the entering in of the gate of Joshua the governor of the city, which were on a man's left hand at the gate of the city. Nevertheless the priests of the high places came not up to the altar of the LORD in Jerusalem, but they did eat of the unleavened bread among their brethren. And he defiled Topheth, which is in the valley of the children of Hinnom, that no man might make his son or his daughter to pass through the fire to Molech. And he took away the horses that the kings of Judah had given to the sun, at the entering in of the house of the LORD, by the chamber of Nathanmelech the chamberlain, which was in the suburbs, and burned the chariots of the sun with fire. And the altars that were on the top of the upper chamber of Ahaz, which the kings of Judah had made, and the altars which Manasseh had made in the two courts of the house of the LORD, did the king beat down, and brake them down from thence, and cast the dust of them into the brook Kidron. And the high places that were before Jerusalem, which were on the right hand of the mount of corruption, which Solomon the king of Israel had builded for Ashtoreth the abomination of the Zidonians, and for Chemosh the abomination of the Moabites, and for Milcom the abomination of the children of Ammon, did the king defile. And he brake in pieces the images, and cut down the groves, and filled their places with the bones of men. Moreover the altar that was at Bethel, and the high place which Jeroboam the son of Nebat, who made Israel to sin, had made, both that altar and the high place he brake down, and burned the high place, and stamped it small to powder, and burned the grove. And as Josiah turned himself, he spied the sepulchres that were there in the mount, and sent, and took the bones out of the sepulchres, and burned them upon the altar, and polluted it, according to the word of the LORD which the man of God proclaimed, who proclaimed these words. Then he said, What title is that that I see? And the men of the city told him, It is the sepulchre of the man of God, which came from Judah, and proclaimed these things that thou hast done against the altar of Bethel. And he said, Let him alone; let no man move his bones. So they let his bones alone, with the bones of the prophet that came out of Samaria. And all the houses also of the high places that were in the cities of Samaria, which the kings of Israel had made to provoke the LORD to anger, Josiah took away, and did to them according to all the acts that he had done in Bethel. And he slew all the priests of the high places that were there upon the altars, and burned men's bones upon them, and returned to Jerusalem.

I have written these things about some of the revelations God gave me through dreams because of the following two reasons:

1. On Thursday, November 3, 2016, God said to me, "Cliff, I showed you a great revelation about this nation and you did nothing about it. What else will I show you for you to know that Trump is the president of the United States?" This time around I do not want to do nothing about it, especially when God has clearly shown me 'what else' on August 15, 2020.

2. My prayers on Saturday, November 5, 2016, when I saw how terrible the polls were against Trump. I prayed as I had never prayed before, and my prayer was, "God, if you make this happen in America, I will go to any length to open the eyes of your people for your people are blind." As we all know, God answered my prayers, He made it happen in 2016. I must keep

my promise to God and go to any length to open the eyes of God's people.

Ephesians 1:15-23

Wherefore I also, after I heard of your faith in the Lord Jesus, and love unto all the saints, Cease not to give thanks for you, making mention of you in my prayers; That the God of our Lord Jesus Christ, the Father of glory, may give unto you the spirit of wisdom and revelation in the knowledge of him: The eyes of your understanding being enlightened; that ye may know what is the hope of his calling, and what the riches of the glory of his inheritance in the saints, And what is the exceeding greatness of his power to us-ward who believe, according to the working of his mighty power, Which he wrought in Christ, when he raised him from the dead, and set him at his own right hand in the heavenly places, Far above all principality, and power, and might, and dominion, and every name that is named, not only in this world, but also in that which is to come: And hath put all things under his feet, and gave him to be the head over all things to the church, Which is his body, the fulness of him that filleth all in all.

My earnest prayers and efforts are for the eyes of understanding of God's people to be opened to understand what God is doing through President Trump for the End Time to understand the exceedingly great power of God moving and working mightily through us who believe, to bring about the ongoing revival of the end time.

May God bless and strengthen President Donald J. Trump for the service God has called him to do in Jesus' mighty name, Amen!

My Fears And Burden

The Deep State, propelled by Satan, has done many things in the book and off the book to silence President Trump politically without success. All their efforts so far have boomeranged and worked in the favor of President Trump and God's people.

Romans 8:28

And we know that all things work together for good to them that love God, to them who are the called according to his purpose.

Since all their wicked works have not silenced President Trump but rather, God has used them to promote him, the most logical question to ask is "What is next?" Will they attempt to assassinate him? I fear because this is a legitimate question. The Deep State does not really have many options left.

Secondly, since all the political persecution and blackmailing strategies by the Deep State against President Trump to keep power have failed miserably, if they choose not to go the route of assassination, or the plot fails, there is another fear, and this one is more conceivable. The Deep State must retain power at all costs to achieve its satanic agendas for the New World Order. Satan is desperate to stop the hand of God, to stop the end-time revival. Since the Deep State knows that they will not be able to retain power through the 2024 election, my fear is that Satan will use President Biden to drag America into war with Russia or Iran to keep power. Then there will be no presidential election because it is unconstitutional to change the commander in chief in time of war. This is a legitimate fear that is conceivable and a move most likely to be made by the Deep State.

Moreso, this fear of war is more real to me because of a dream I once had. In 2005 while I was still in Nigeria, I had a dream where I was in a foreign country and this country was devastated by war. Buildings and cars were burnt, and dead bodies were on the streets. The lawns were all burned or dried up. I was walking on the streets preaching the gospel and life began to come back. As I preached, dead bodies began to come back to life and the lawns began to turn green again, then I woke up. The foreign country I came to and have remained in is the United States of America. I do not know what this dream meant, but I hope and pray that war does not break out in America, neither civil nor foreign.

The children of God in America and all over the world must take up this burden of prayers with me. God has revealed His will, but we must pray against the devices of Satan.

2Corinthians 2:11

Lest Satan should get an advantage of us: for we are not ignorant of his devices.

We must repent from our wicked (sinful) ways against God and call upon Him for mercy for our sake, the nation, and for generations unborn.

2Chronicles 7:14-15

If my people, which are called by my name, shall humble themselves, and pray, and seek my face, and turn from their wicked ways; then will I hear from heaven, and will forgive their sin, and will heal their land. Now mine eyes shall be open, and mine ears attent unto the prayer that is made in this place.

Please join prayer warriors every Sunday for the next year as we pray in President Trump and the will of God in America and the world. Prayers started on Sunday, November 5, 2023, to end November 2024, after the US presidential election.

Zoom ID: 86153809145,
Time: 8:30 pm EST.

May God bless you abundantly as you join to carry this burden for the Lord.

Chapter 8

How Close Is The Imminent Return
Of Jesus Christ:
How Close Is The End?

The fact that we are living in the last days cannot be disputed by any rational mind. Knowing that we are living in the last days, Christians must live and walk circumspectly (watchful, restrained, and prudent). However, the issue is, how convinced are Christians that our redemption is nearer than when we first believed and that there is no continuing city. How prepared are we for the sound of the trumpet?

Romans 13:11

And that, knowing the time, that now it is high time to awake out of sleep: for now is our salvation nearer than when we believed.

Hebrews 13:13-14

Let us go forth therefore unto him without the camp, bearing his reproach. For here have we no continuing city, but we seek one to come.

Biblical Signs of the Last Days:

There are many signs of the last days stated in the Bible. Among these are six major signs of the end time. They are:

(1) Deception

(2) Abounding of Lawlessness

(3) Great Tribulation

(4) Progressive and Normalcy of Life Amidst Perilous Time

(5) Gospel Preached in all the World

(6) The Fig Tree

Deception:

The last days will be characterized by deception. This is the very first warning Jesus gave when asked for the sign of His coming and the end times by His disciples. Deception in the last days will be the singular most detrimental sign of the last days to believers. The deception of the last days through great signs, lying wonders, and the spirit of "It Does not Matter", will damn more believers' souls in hell than any other thing. This is why Jesus forewarned that believers should pay earnest attention to deception. The Church today is filled with apostasy. Many are deceived by their denominational doctrines of demons and others, by the lack of sound biblical doctrines, that is the doctrine of no doctrines – Christianity as it seems good to you.

Matthew 24:2-5,11

And as he sat upon the mount of Olives, the disciples came unto him privately, saying, Tell us, when shall these things be? and what shall be the sign of thy coming, and of the end of the world? And Jesus answered and said unto them, Take heed that no man deceive you. For many shall come in my name, saying, I am Christ; and shall deceive many. And many false prophets shall rise, and shall deceive many.

The deception of the last days will be pioneered by false-Christs and false prophets. The deception and manipulations of these false prophets and false-Christs through signs and lying wonders will be great and able to deceive even the elect.

Matthew 24:24

For false christs and false prophets will rise and show great signs and wonders to deceive, if possible, even the elect.

The elects are the genuinely born-again Christians with the Spirit of God whom God through His foreknowledge has chosen to dwell with Him in heaven forever. These are the people that Jesus spoke to saying,

John 14:2-3

In My Father's house are many mansions; if it were not so, I would have told you. I go to prepare a place for you. And if I go and prepare a place for you, I will come again and receive you to Myself; that where I am, there you may be also.

Jesus said born-again, sanctified, Holy Ghost-filled Christians will get caught up in Satan's deception of the last days through signs, and lying wonders and miss eternal life. All that is needed to send a genuine Christian to hell is one error. Therefore, for your soul's sake be watchful, study the Bible daily, and be prayerful against deception.

2 Thesselonians 2:9-12

Even him, whose coming is after the working of Satan with all power and signs and lying wonders, And with all deceivableness of unrighteousness in them that perish; because they received not the love of the truth, that they might be saved. And for this cause God shall send them strong delusion, that they should believe a lie: That they all might be damned who believed not the truth, but had pleasure in unrighteousness.

Most times, Christians who started well get caught up in the web of deception, being deceived and deceiving others because they want to be accepted by all. They covet the prosperity of false prophets according to the world's standard. They view prosperity in Ministry by how famous, how rich, the attendance in service and how many branches the Ministry has. They measure prosperity in Ministry by worldly standards and not according to God's standard, which is how many are holy and heaven-ready. As a Christian, Choir leader, Minister, Pastor, Prophet, Reverend, Bishop, General Overseer, General Superintendent or whatever your title may be; "Please, reject the prosperity of fools and resist the pressure to be accepted by all!" Stand only on the perfect truth of the Scripture no matter how hard or unpopular it may be, that is, the Word of God. The Bible says that it is only false prophets that are accepted by all.

Luke 6:26

Woe unto you, when all men shall speak well of you! for so did their fathers to the false prophets.

Remember the sermon of our Master and Savior Jesus Christ in the synagogue of Capernaum.

John 6:43-44,60-61-63,65-68

Jesus therefore answered and said unto them, Murmur not among yourselves. No man can come to me, except the Father which hath sent me draw him: and I will raise him up at the last day. Many therefore of his disciples, when they had heard this, said, This is an hard saying; who can hear it? When Jesus knew in himself that his disciples murmured at it, he said unto them, Doth this offend you? What and if ye shall see the Son of man ascend up where he was before? It is the spirit that quickeneth; the flesh profiteth nothing: the words that I speak unto you, they are spirit, and they are life. And he said, Therefore said I unto you, that no man can come unto me, except it were given unto him of my Father. From that time many of his disciples went back, and walked no more with him. Then said Jesus unto the twelve, Will ye also go away? Then Simon Peter answered him, Lord, to whom shall we go? thou hast the words of eternal life.

Many of Jesus' disciples were offended by His sermon and said it is a hard saying. The word of God has a lot of hard sayings that must be obeyed to produce the holiness for eternal life.

2Peter 3:16

as also in all his epistles, speaking in them of these things, in which are some things hard to understand, which untaught and unstable people twist to their own destruction, as they do also the rest of the Scriptures.

Jesus declared to them that it is the Spirit of God that gives life and the words He speaks are Spirit and are life. So is every word of God that proceeds from the mouth of a Christian – they are life-giving Spirit. Jesus did not plead with His departing disciples to stay, neither did He dilute the Word to accommodate them. Rather He turned to the twelve that remained and asked them if they also wanted to leave like the vast majority. Peter's response clearly shows what keeps true believers in church – the Word of God. Therefore, preach the word of God without fear or favor. True believers whom the Father has drawn for eternal life will rejoice, while the children of disobedient Satan, reserved for eternal damnation in hell, will be offended.

Therefore, be careful not to get caught up and be entangled in the deception of these last days.

Abounding of Lawlessness:

To abound means to exist in great measure, to be full of. Therefore, the last days will be full of lawlessness. Lawlessness is not abiding by the laws of God. It simply means sin.

1 John 3:4

Whosoever committeth sin transgresseth also the law: for sin is the transgression of the law.

Therefore, the last days will be characterized by an abundance of sin. It will be a period when good will be taken for evil and evil will be glamorized and called good. If you look at the world and the churches today, you will see an abundance of lawlessness. The lawlessness of the world has been glamorized by Hollywood and through social media and adopted by believers in the churches. People despise the laws of God and loathe scriptural godly boundaries because they want to live an indulgent life. As a result, the love of many has grown cold. This perfectly characterizes the 21st Century world – the last days.

Matthew 24:12-13

And because iniquity shall abound, the love of many shall wax cold. But he that shall endure unto the end, the same shall be saved.

2 Thessalonians 2:7

For the mystery of iniquity doth already work: only he who now letteth will let, until he be taken out of the way.

Because the mystery of lawlessness is already at work, as a sign of the last days, people no longer endure sound doctrine. They have become self-centered, driven by self-pleasure and achievements, loving themselves even above God. The abundance of lawlessness will lead to Perilous times in the last days. Perilous times means dangerous or hazardous times, a period with grave risk in living. Many people will profess to be godly but deny the power of godliness which is holiness.

2 Timothy 3:1-5

This know also, that in the last days perilous times shall come. For men shall be lovers of their own selves, covetous, boasters, proud, blasphemers, disobedient to parents, unthankful, unholy, Without natural affection, trucebreakers, false accusers, incontinent, fierce, despisers of those that are good, Traitors, heady, highminded, lovers of pleasures more than lovers of God; Having a form of godliness, but denying the power thereof: from such turn away.

Scoffers will rise in the last days because they want to live an indulgent life of lawlessness. They will mock sound biblical doctrines, laugh at the mention of the biblical signs of the last days saying that these things have been happening since the existence of the earth and Christ has not come. They will laugh at the message of Christ's imminent return and say we have been hearing of this for a long time now and life has continued as the same.

2Peter 3:3-4

Knowing this first, that there shall come in the last days scoffers, walking after their own lusts, And saying, Where is the promise of his coming? for since the fathers fell asleep, all things continue as they were from the beginning of the creation.

Great Tribulation:

Tribulation means grievous trouble and severe suffering. This great tribulation will be caused by wars and rumors of wars, famine, pestilences, and natural disasters. There will be great tribulation such as have never been seen since the beginning of the world.

Matthew 24:6-8,21-22

And you will hear of wars and rumors of wars. See that you are not troubled; for all these things must come to pass, but the end is not yet. For nation will rise against nation, and kingdom against kingdom. And there will be famines, pestilences, and earthquakes in various places. All these are the beginning of sorrows. For then there will be great tribulation, such as has not been since the beginning of the world until this time, no, nor ever shall be.

You do not have to look very far to see, hear, or witness wars and rumors of wars, famine, pestilences, and natural disasters of proportions never witnessed before. There is literally no geopolitical zone in the world where there is no war and rumor of war. The West and America are in a proxy war with Russia in Ukraine. Israel and Palestine are at war in the Middle East. Africa and Asia are boiling with various kinds of wars. Every day there are rumors of war here and there, China is planning to invade Taiwan. Similarly, natural disasters and pestilences all over the world have increased at alarming proportions. Do we talk about wildfires, earthquakes, or floods? These things are now happening at unprecedented proportions and rates. The world just went through a global shutdown because of Covid19 and President Biden and his associates are planning to introduce another. The evidence of the last days is blatantly before us, even the blind can see them.

Progressive and Normalcy of Life Amidst Perilous Time:

One amazing thing about the End-Time as recorded in the Scripture is that amidst all the chaos of the end-time, deception, abounding of lawlessness, great tribulations of wars, rumors of war, pestilences, and natural disasters, the world will not be alarmed. They will continue to live life as normal. They will only be filled with progressive ideas and the pursuit of their self-loving, indulgent life of pleasure. You can see these things for yourself. Despite Ukrainian lives being decimated at an alarming rate in the US-NATO proxy war against Russia in Ukraine, it is widely reported in the news media that nightlife in the club is still booming in Ukraine. The world will continue life as normal as if nothing is going on; marriages, partying, and planning for the next great achievement without any consideration of the terrible turn of events in the world. Jesus warned that when we see these things happening, we should know that the end is at the door.

Matthew 24:33-34

So likewise ye, when ye shall see all these things, know that it is near, even at the doors. Verily I say unto you, This generation shall not pass, till all these things be fulfilled.

However, the world will not heed. They will continue life as normal and ignore all the warning signs until that day take them by surprise just like in the days of Noah.

Matthew 24:37-39

But as the days of Noe were, so shall also the coming of the Son of man be. For as in the days that were before the flood they were eating and drinking, marrying and giving in marriage, until the day that Noe entered into the ark, And knew not until the flood came, and took them all away; so shall also the coming of the Son of man be.

The Gospel Preached In all The World:

Another sign of the end time is that the gospel will be preached to the ends of the world as a witness so that none shall have an excuse. Since the advent of the internet, the gospel of our Lord and Savior Jesus Christ is now able to reach places that were previously hard to reach. Many are now motivated to preach the gospel through social media for all the right reasons and wrong reasons. Some because they have compassion for lost souls and are truly called by God to reach them, while others preach the gospel there for the sake of money, and fame; the god that called them is their belly.

Philippians 3:18-19

(For many walk, of whom I have told you often, and now tell you even weeping, that they are the enemies of the cross of Christ: Whose end is destruction, whose God is their belly, and whose glory is in their shame, who mind earthly things.)

Nevertheless, all things work together for the good of God's plan for His people.

Romans 8:28

And we know that all things work together for good to them that love God, to them who are the called according to his purpose.

Apostle Paul being fully aware of this stated:

Philippians 1:15-18

Some indeed preach Christ even of envy and strife; and some also of good will: The one preach Christ of contention, not sincerely, supposing to add affliction to my bonds: But the other of love, knowing that I am set for the defence of the gospel. What then? notwithstanding, every way, whether in pretence, or in truth, Christ is preached; and I therein do rejoice, yea, and will rejoice.

Whatever may be the motivation for anyone preaching the gospel through social media and through the conventional way, the truth is that the gospel is being preached via social media powered by the internet. The gospel of Jesus Christ is reaching the ends of the world at an ultra-speed. Therefore, the wise get the message that the end is at hand.

Matthew 24:14

And this gospel of the kingdom shall be preached in all the world for a witness unto all nations; and then shall the end come.

The Fig Tree & All The Trees:

Luke 21:29 -32

And he spake to them a parable; Behold the fig tree, and all the trees; When they now shoot forth, ye see and know of your own selves that summer is now nigh at hand. So likewise ye, when ye see these things come to pass, know ye that the kingdom of God is nigh at hand. Verily I say unto you, This generation shall not pass away, till all be fulfilled.

Jesus spoke to us His disciples saying that in the same way we can know that summer is at hand when we observe that the trees are beginning to blossom. In the same manner, we should also be able to know that the end is at hand when we see these signs: wars, rumors of wars, famine, pestilences, and natural disasters of unprecedented proportions. When we observe the normalcy of life in the world amidst this terrible turn of events, when we observe that the gospel is being preached to the ends of the world, then we should know that the end is at the doorstep; and that the generation witnessing these things shall not pass away before the imminent return of Jesus Christ.

Knowing that the end is at hand, everyone must repent of their sins and turn to Jesus Christ for salvation. Christians must repent of their sins and perfect holiness inwardly and outwardly. God is merciful, and it is not His will that anyone should perish. However, we must seek Him while He may be found. We must seek His mercies before it is too late. If we repent and seek His mercy, He will abundantly pardon.

Isaiah 55:6-7

Seek ye the LORD while he may be found, call ye upon him while he is near: Let the wicked forsake his way, and the unrighteous man his thoughts: and let him return unto the LORD, and he will have mercy upon him; and to our God, for he will abundantly pardon.

2Chronicles 7:14

If my people, which are called by my name, shall humble themselves, and pray, and seek my face, and turn from their wicked ways; then will I hear from heaven, and will forgive their sin, and will heal their land.

Chapter 9

Trump The Protagonist For The Fig Tree Metaphor

The book of Luke metaphorically refers to the fig tree and other trees to be a sign of the End-Time.

Luke 21:29

And he spake to them a parable; Behold the fig tree, and all the trees;

However, the book of Matthew only used the fig tree for its end time metaphor. All other trees were not included.

Matthew 24:32-34

Now learn a parable of the fig tree; When his branch is yet tender, and putteth forth leaves, ye know that summer is nigh: So likewise ye, when ye shall see all these things, know that it is near, even at the doors. Verily I say unto you, This generation shall not pass, till all these things be fulfilled.

Many eschatologists interpret this fig tree metaphor in Matthew to symbolize Israel. Their interpretation is that when the fig tree, that is, Israel, begins to form again as a nation, we should know that the end is at hand and that generation will not pass before the rapture and second coming of Jesus Christ.

The Fig Tree As Israel And
The Role Trump Played

Let us examine the fig tree metaphor as a symbol for Israel. Israel was first made desolate by the Babylonian kingdom around 587 BC because they forsook their God.

2kings 25:1-2,8-12

And it came to pass in the ninth year of his reign, in the tenth month, in the tenth day of the month, that Nebuchadnezzar king of Babylon came, he, and all his host, against Jerusalem, and pitched against it; and they built forts against it round about. And the city was besieged unto the eleventh year of king Zedekiah. And in the fifth month, on the seventh day of the month, which is the nineteenth year of king Nebuchadnezzar king of Babylon, came Nebuzaradan, captain of the guard, a servant of the king of Babylon, unto Jerusalem: And he burnt the house of the LORD, and the king's house, and all the houses of Jerusalem, and every great man's house burnt he with fire. And all the army of the Chaldees, that were with the captain of the guard, brake down the walls of Jerusalem round about. Now the rest of the people that were left in the city, and the fugitives that fell away to the king of Babylon, with the remnant of the multitude, did Nebuzaradan the captain of the guard carry away. But the captain of the guard left of the poor of the land to be vinedressers and husbandmen.

For Jesus to come for the first time Israel had to return to their land as a nation because the Messiah had to be born in Israel with Jerusalem as its capital. To accomplish this, God raised a man – King Cyrus whom He prophesied of through Isaiah about 150 years before he was born. God declared that Cyrus would build the city of Jerusalem and release Israel from captivity.

Issaiah 45:1,4-6,13

Thus saith the LORD to his anointed, to Cyrus, whose right hand I have holden, to subdue nations before him; and I will loose the loins of kings, to open before him the two leaved gates; and the gates shall not be shut; For Jacob my servant's sake, and Israel mine elect, I have even called thee by thy name: I have surnamed thee, though thou hast not known me. I am the LORD, and there is none else, there is no God beside me: I girded thee, though thou hast not known me: That they may know from the rising of the sun, and from the west, that there is none beside me. I am the LORD, and there is none else. I have raised him up in righteousness, and I will direct all his ways: he shall build my city, and he shall let go my captives, not for price nor reward, saith the LORD of hosts.

This task was accomplished by King Cyrus as God foretold all for the purpose of the first coming of Jesus. Jerusalem was rebuilt, Israelites returned to their land, and Jesus was born. Jesus was the Messiah to save Israel from sin, deliver her from her enemies' roundabout, and give them lasting peace. However, the Jews rejected Jesus because He came as a harmless lamb, preaching repentance and peace. From their perspective, He died as a weakling on the cross. They were expecting a warrior, a king who would raise an army to fight and deliver Israel from all her enemies.

This was a grievous error on the part of the Jews. They were too blind to discern their savior and salvation even when the nature, character, suffering, death, and resurrection of the Messiah was written all over the Scripture. If Israel had repented and accepted Jesus, there would have been unending peace in the Middle East. If Israel had repented and embraced Jesus and His gospel of peace, they would have evangelized that whole region and united the children of Abraham before Islam came to divide them, and plant bitterness and enmity.

Islam was born about six hundred (600) years after the death and resurrection of Jesus Christ. Six hundred years would have been enough to Christianize the Middle East and the world simultaneously. The Middle East would have been the hub of the Gospel and Christianity. They would have loved each other with the love of Christ and exported the same to the whole world.

Luke 24:46-47

And said unto them, Thus it is written, and thus it behoved Christ to suffer, and to rise from the dead the third day: And that repentance and remission of sins should be preached in his name among all nations, beginning at Jerusalem.

Israel's rejection of Jesus Christ their Messiah gave occasion to Satan, which resulted in an unending bitter conflict in the Middle East. A conflict that will only get worse and fiercer until the second coming of Jesus Christ. Secondly, their rejection of Jesus Christ resulted in their second desolation because they rejected their God again, their Messiah Jesus Christ. Jesus said to them that their house would be left to them desolate. Therefore, in 70AD the Roman Empire decimated Israel and they were scattered throughout the whole world, mostly Europe.

Matt 23:37-38

O Jerusalem, Jerusalem, thou that killest the prophets, and stonest them which are sent unto thee, how often would I have gathered thy children together, even as a hen gathereth her chickens under her wings, and ye would not! Behold, your house is left unto you desolate. For I say unto you, Ye shall not see me henceforth, till ye shall say, Blessed is he that cometh in the name of the Lord.

This resulted in the mass annihilation of the Jews by Adolf Hitler during the holocaust that spanned between 1933 to 1945. Then after the end of the Second World War in 1945. The United States of America under the leadership of President Harry S. Truman facilitated the creation of the State of Israel on May 14, 1948, in support of the Zionist Movement led by David Ben-Gurion at that time. The creation of the State of Israel in 1948 is interpreted by many eschatologists to be the blossoming of the fig tree as spoken by Jesus.

Matthew 24:32-34

Now learn a parable of the fig tree; When his branch is yet tender, and putteth forth leaves, ye know that summer is nigh: So likewise ye, when ye shall see all these things, know that it is near, even at the doors. Verily I say unto you, This generation shall not pass, till all these things be fulfilled.

Since the formation of the nation of Israel in 1948, Tel Aviv, not Jerusalem, was its capital, and Israel was not in full control of the Golan Heights. Although the United States acknowledged internally that Jerusalem should belong to Israel as its capital. However, no United States president after President Harry S. Truman, had enough courage to officially acknowledge and endorse it. They were all afraid that it might cause World War III, or something close. Nevertheless, when the man God has chosen, President Donald J. Trump came to power in 2017, he officially recognized Jerusalem as the eternal capital of Israel that same year and moved the American Embassy in Tel Aviv to Jerusalem.

President Trump also officially recognized Israel's sovereignty over the Golan Heights, something that could not be done for over fifty-eight years. If the start of Israel as a nation symbolizes the blossoming of the fig tree, then for the fig tree, that is, Israel to fully blossom, Israel must have Jerusalem as its capital and be in full control of all its territories. This was accomplished in 2017 by President Trump during his first term in office.

President Trump became the protagonist for the full blossoming of the fig tree-Israel as chosen by God, just like King Cyrus. Israel as the fig tree interpretation of Matthew 24:32-34 and its fulfilment also accurately shows that we are at the end. This can be said because the generation born at the start of the blossoming is at the end of life. This was also accomplished by President Trump in preparation for the second coming of Jesus Christ as King Cyrus did for His first coming.

Issaiah 45:1,4-6,13

Thus saith the LORD to his anointed, to Cyrus (TRUMP), whose right hand I have holden, to subdue nations before him; and I will loose the loins of kings, to open before him the two leaved gates; and the gates shall not be shut; For Jacob my servant's sake, and Israel mine elect, I have even called thee by thy name: I have surnamed thee, though thou hast not known me. I am the LORD, and there is none else, there is no God beside me: I girded thee, though thou hast not known me: That they may know from the rising of the sun, and from the west, that there is none beside me. I am the LORD, and there is none else. I have raised him up in righteousness, and I will direct all his ways: he shall build my city, and he shall let go my captives, not for price nor reward, saith the LORD of hosts.

Jesus said that the generation that witnesses the blossoming of the fig tree shall not pass away before His second coming.

Matthew 24:32

Verily I say unto you, This generation shall not pass, till all these things be fulfilled.

According to the interpretation of these eschatologists, if the fig tree stands for Israel, then the fig tree-Israel began to blossom in 1948. The generation that witnessed the blossoming of the fig tree-Israel are those born in 1948. Those born in 1948 are 75 years old this 2023. They are at the end of life and will all soon pass away. Nevertheless, Jesus said that they all will not pass away before everything He said about the end, including the rapture and His second coming are fulfilled. Therefore, if that generation is at its end and does not have much time left, how much time do you think is left before the rapture and Jesus's second coming? How many of them will still be alive by 2030 at 82 years? Think! They will not all pass away before the rapture.

Chapter 10
Trump The Protagonist For The Rapture

1 Corinthians 15:51

Behold, I shew you a mystery; We shall not all sleep, but we shall all be changed, In a moment, in the twinkling of an eye, at the last trump: for the trumpet shall sound, and the dead shall be raised incorruptible, and we shall be changed.

The colon (:) dividing the sentence in 1Corinthians 15:52 represents a major division to indicate that what follows is an implication or elaboration of what preceded.

1 Corinthians 15:52

In a moment, in the twinkling of an eye, at the last trump: for the trumpet shall sound, and the dead shall be raised incorruptible, and we shall be changed.

If an elaboration, then the trump is the same as the trumpet. If an implication, then the trump is different from the trumpet, and the sounding of the Trumpet will be the implication for the last trump. (for example, (1) At the class: evolution shall be discussed. (2) At the meeting: food will be served.) In these two sentences the colons (:) indicate that what followed is either an elaboration or an implication of what preceded. It is clearly not an elaboration because we can see that what followed are different subjects from what preceded.

In these examples, we understand that the class and the meeting are not the same thing as evolution and food. Therefore, we can accurately conclude that what followed the colons are implications for what preceded them. The discussion on evolution is the implication, that is, the resulting event of the class. The same is with the serving of food as a different event that will result from the meeting. What then is the last trump in 1Corinthians 15:52?

1Corinthians 15:52

In a moment, in the twinkling of an eye, at the last trump: for the trumpet shall sound, and the dead shall be raised incorruptible, and we shall be changed.

A. The Last Trump Is The Trumpet (elaboration)

Using the elaboration scenario, the "last trump" is the same as the trumpet. The verse can then be interpreted to mean that, at the last trump (trumpet): the trumpet shall sound. Meaning that the trumpet will sound more than once, and then at the last sound of the trumpet the dead and living saints will be raptured.

1Thess 4:15-17

For this we say unto you by the word of the Lord, that we which are alive and remain unto the coming of the Lord shall not prevent them which are asleep. For the Lord himself shall descend from heaven with a shout, with the voice of the archangel, and with the trump of God: and the dead in Christ shall rise first: Then we which are alive and remain shall be caught up together with them in the clouds, to meet the Lord in the air: and so shall we ever be with the Lord.

B. The Last Trump Is An Awakening Sign (implication).

It could mean that the "last trump" is a metaphor for the last sign or maybe the last awakening (alarm, warning) before the trumpet sounds. This means that the trump is different from the trumpet and the trumpet will be the resulting effect of the last trump. Then could it be the coronavirus pandemic, which had a resemblance to the rapture and after-rapture event? The world was under lockdown as if the rapture had taken place as the world's governments were trying to provide answers and solutions for the phenomenon that just took place. People could not go into the stores and markets to buy or sell unless they had their masks (mark) on. People could not travel except if they had their Covid 19 vaccination certificate (mark) or negative test certificate (mark). Could this be the last sign or last awakening before rapture?

Matt 24:7

For nation shall rise against nation, and kingdom against kingdom: and there shall be famines, and pestilences, and earthquakes, in divers places.

Revelation 13:16-17

And he causeth all, both small and great, rich and poor, free and bond, to receive a mark in their right hand, or in their foreheads:

And that no man might buy or sell, save he that had the mark, or the name of the beast, or the number of his name.

C. The Last Trump Is President Trump (implication)

God does not use words carelessly. Every word and figure in the Scripture were carefully chosen by God and are filled with mysteries. In every word and figure of the Bible abides knowledge, understanding, and wisdom. The ability to decode and accurately interpret their meaning with the help of the Spirit of God gives knowledge and revelation of things present and things to come. The fact that these are the last days is clearly seen by the blind and understood by the cognitively impaired. Only the fools can neither see it nor understand it.

Man cannot be able to fully uncover all the mysteries hidden in the Bible in all his existence. The seven-day creation account in the Bible holds a lot of mysteries to understanding the life span of the world and the end of all things. God created the world in seven days and rested on the seventh day Sabbath.

Genesis 2:1-2

Thus the heavens and the earth were finished, and all the host of them. And on the seventh day God ended his work which he had made; and he rested on the seventh day from all his work which he had made.

The Bible gave us a literal seven-day creation account in which God rested on the seventh day. However, the Bible also reveals that one day is like one thousand years with the Lord. And this biblical truth is evident in these Scriptures.

Psalms 90:3-4

Thou turnest man to destruction; and sayest, Return, ye children of men. For a thousand years in thy sight are but as yesterday when it is past, and as a watch in the night.

2Peter 3:8-10

But, beloved, be not ignorant of this one thing, that one day is with the Lord as a thousand years, and a thousand years as one day. The Lord is not slack concerning his promise, as some men count slackness; but is longsuffering to us-ward, not willing that any should perish, but that all should come to repentance. But the day of the Lord will come as a thief in the night; in the which the heavens shall pass away with a great noise, and the elements shall melt with fervent heat, the earth also and the works that are therein shall be burned up.

According to Scripture, one thousand years equals one 24-hour day in the eyes of the Lord. The seven days of creation also represent the seven thousand years of man's existence. The world has been on a seven-day journey of existence and is currently on the sixth day. God has used this principle to code Bible revelations to man about the end of time. To better understand that one day of the Lord equals one thousand years, we go to the account of Adam. God instructed Adam not to eat of the Tree of Knowledge of Good and Evil because he will die the day, he eats it.

Genesis 2:17

But of the tree of the knowledge of good and evil, thou shalt not eat of it: for in the day that thou eatest thereof thou shalt surely die.

Man was created to live forever, but when he sinned by disobeying God's commandment, he died that same day according to the word of the Lord. Now remember that a day to the Lord is a thousand years. Adam died at the age of 930 years, which is within the same day that he ate the fruit in the eyes of the Lord. Since then, no man has ever lived more than one day in the eyes of the Lord. Methuselah, who lived the longest since the history of man, died at the age of 969 years. He died within one day in the eyes of the Lord. No man has been able to live beyond one day according to the word of the Lord.

Genesis 5:3

And Adam lived an hundred and thirty years, and begat a son in his own likeness, after his image; and called his name Seth:

Genesis 5:27

And all the days of Methuselah were nine hundred sixty and nine years: and he died.

From the creation of Adam to the coming of Jesus Christ is about four days, that is, four thousand years in the eyes of man. The earth is still in its second day from the coming of Jesus Christ to this day. That is to say that from the death and resurrection of Jesus Christ to this day is less than two thousand years. Jesus was born around 3BC, died, and resurrected around 33AD. Counting from His death and resurrection to 2023 is about one thousand nine hundred and ninety years (1,990). From the creation of Adam, the world has existed for about six thousand years. In the eyes of the Lord, the world is in its sixth day of existence.

The Bible tells us that the days of man are few and full of trouble.

Job 14:1

Man that is born of a woman is of few days, and full of trouble.

The Bible also reveals that God will deliver His own from six troubles and in the seventh, no evil will touch him.

Job 14:1; 5:19

Man that is born of a woman is of few days, and full of trouble. He shall deliver thee in six troubles: yea, in seven there shall no evil touch thee.

It is the days of man that brings trouble to him, and God is saying that He will deliver His own from the troubles of six days and on the seventh day he will be free from evil. Man has existed for troublesome six thousand years, that is, six days in God's eyes. In these six days, God has continually delivered His own from the troubles of the day and promised to keep him free from trouble on the seventh day. The seventh day is the Sabbath, a day of rest from all troubles, God rested from all His work on the Sabbath day. The seventh day, which is the last one thousand years is going to be a day free from all evil. That is a thousand years free from all evil, which is referred to as the millennial reign of Christ.

Hebrews 4:1,4-5,8-10

Let us therefore fear, lest, a promise being left us of entering into his rest, any of you should seem to come short of it. For he spake in a certain place of the seventh day on this wise, And God did rest the seventh day from all his works. And in this place again, If they shall enter into my rest. For if Jesus had given them rest, then would he not afterward have spoken of another day. There remaineth therefore a rest to the people of God. For he that is entered into his rest, he also hath ceased from his own works, as God did from his.

Revelations 20:5-6

But the rest of the dead lived not again until the thousand years were finished. This is the first resurrection. Blessed and holy is he that hath part in the first resurrection: on such the second death hath no power, but they shall be priests of God and of Christ, and shall reign with him a thousand years.

The Bible undoubtedly states that there will be the first resurrection and those who were part of the first resurrection are holy and will reign with Christ for a thousand years. This indicates that the first resurrection will take place at the end of the sixth day because Christ will reign on the last day – the seventh day. The seventh day is the earth's Sabbath day, God will give the earth rest from all evil. It will be a thousand years of Christ's reign on earth without the presence of evil in any form or shape. The world is almost at the end of the sixth day. There are just about seven to ten years left to the end of the sixth day before the first resurrection takes place. Man is in his sixth day of existence, that is, the second day since the time of Jesus Christ. Prophet Hosea was a man whom God used as a sign to Israel. God used him to demonstrate Israel's whoredom, and God's love for them and to communicate His coming judgment. What did God communicate to His children through Hosea about His coming to rescue His children?

Hosea 6:1-2

Come, and let us return unto the LORD: for he hath torn, and he will heal us; he hath smitten, and he will bind us up. After two days will he revive us: in the third day he will raise us up, and we shall live in his sight.

These verses communicate the return of sinners to Christ, the Christian revival that has been going on for two days (2,000 years), and the first resurrection. The communicate that God will continue to have mercy on sinners who return to Him and continue to revive the world for two days (2,000 years). Then on the third day, He will raise up those that were revived to live in His presence forever.

1 Theselonians 4:15-17,

For this we say unto you by the word of the Lord, that we which are alive and remain unto the coming of the Lord shall not prevent them which are asleep. For the Lord himself shall descend from heaven with a shout, with the voice of the archangel, and with the trump of God: and the dead in Christ shall rise first: Then we which are alive and remain shall be caught up together with them in the clouds, to meet the Lord in the air: and so shall we ever be with the Lord.

Revelations 20:5-6

But the rest of the dead lived not again until the thousand years were finished. This is the first resurrection. Blessed and holy is he that hath part in the first resurrection: on such the second death hath no power, but they shall be priests of God and of Christ, and shall reign with him a thousand years.

After two days (2,000 years) of the Christian revival, and the Church age, Christ will return to raise His bride up (The Church: those washed in His blood that kept their garment spotless, holy Christians). The date of Christ's death and resurrection is around 30AD - 33AD which marked the birth of the Church – the Christian revival. From that period to 2023 is about 1,987 to 1,990 years, meaning we are still in the second day of revival (1,000 years as a day to the Lord). This means we have between 7 to 10 years left to the end of the 2 days (2,000 years) of revival. Therefore, the second day of revival will end around the years 2030 to 2033.

What Has President Trump Got To Do With This?

Remember that God does not use words carelessly. Every word and figure in the Bible are significant to understanding what the Spirit of God is communicating to man concerning present and future events.

1 Corinthians 15:52

In a moment, in the twinkling of an eye, at the last trump: for the trumpet shall sound, and the dead shall be raised incorruptible, and we shall be changed.

Using the implication approach, could the "last trump" be metaphorically speaking of President Trump? Could it be saying that the reign of President Trump will be a sign for His imminent return to rapture the Church? Could it be saying that the trumpet will sound after the reign of Trump? Is it just a coincidence that God gave us President Trump, a name synonymous with the last alert for the Rapture as the president of the United States in this undisputable last-days generation? Could it be a coincidence that his second term presidency will end in 2029 right about the close of the second day (2,000 years) of God's revival since Christ's death and resurrection? Was it a coincidence that he was the 45th president and played the same role in restoring Jerusalem as King Cyrus in Isaiah 45? Could God have given us a clue? Is President Trump the protagonist of the end-time? Or is he simply Trump The Great?

I will leave you to draw your own conclusions.

www.ingramcontent.com/pod-product-compliance
Lightning Source LLC
Chambersburg PA
CBHW060339130626
46553CB00003B/1052

*9 7 9 8 9 8 9 6 4 0 8 1 2 *